Star Quilt Designs

Doreen L. Saunders

DOVER PUBLICATIONS, INC., NEW YORK

Copyright © 1991 by Dover Publications, Inc.
All rights reserved under Pan American and International Copyright Conventions.

Published in Canada by General Publishing Company, Ltd., 30 Lesmill Road, Don Mills, Toronto, Ontario.
Published in the United Kingdom by Constable and Company, Ltd., 3 The Lanchesters, 162–164 Fulham Palace Road, London W6 9ER.

Star Quilt Designs is a new work, first published by Dover Publications, Inc., in 1991.

DOVER *Pictorial Archive* SERIES

This book belongs to the Dover Pictorial Archive Series. You may use the designs and illustrations for graphics and crafts applications, free and without special permission, provided that you include no more than four in the same publication or project. (For permission for additional use, please write to Dover Publications, Inc., 31 East 2nd Street, Mineola, N.Y. 11501.)
However, republication or reproduction of any illustration by any other graphic service, whether it be in a book or in any other design resource, is strictly prohibited.

Manufactured in the United States of America
Dover Publications, Inc., 31 East 2nd Street, Mineola, N.Y. 11501

Library of Congress Cataloging-in-Publication Data

Saunders, Doreen Lynn.
    Star quilt designs / by Doreen L. Saunders.
      p.   cm.— (Dover pictorial archive series)
    ISBN 0-486-26912-4 (pbk.)
    1. Patchwork—Patterns. 2. Patchwork quilts—United States.   I. Title.
II. Series.
TT835.S273   1991
746.9′7041—dc20   91-30063
                                                                                                   CIP

Introduction

THAT THE STARS hold a great deal of fascination for us is readily apparent. We make our wishes on a star, hitch our wagons to a star, see our fates written in the stars and thank our lucky stars for our good fortune. Stars were chosen to symbolize the new United States of America and its member states and the imagery of many of the world's religions makes use of stars. With all of this interest in the heavens, it is hardly surprising that star patterns are among the most popular patchwork quilt patterns.

There are dozens of different patterns ranging from the simple Eight-Pointed Star, made up of squares and right triangles, to the intricate Star of Bethlehem with its hundreds of small diamonds. Piecing *this* complex pattern is considered a true test of a quilter's skill.

The names given to these patterns can be political, such as Liberty Star or Texas Lone Star; religious, such as Star of Bethlehem; personal, such as Grandmother's Star or Lucinda's Star; or historical, such as Le Moyne Star (named for the founder of the first permanent settlement in the French territory of Louisiana).

As quiltmakers moved across the country, the names of their quilt patterns were changed to reflect changing circumstances. Thus a single pattern can be known by several different names. For example, the Star of Bethlehem became the Lone Star; Variable Stars turned into Ohio Stars; and Le Moyne Stars changed to Lemon Stars. Conversely, a single name might refer to several different star patterns.

Here, you will find a galaxy of star quilts to spark your imagination and creativity. The design variations possible are truly astounding, as is amply demonstrated by the beautiful quilts shown in these pages.

Lone Star

1

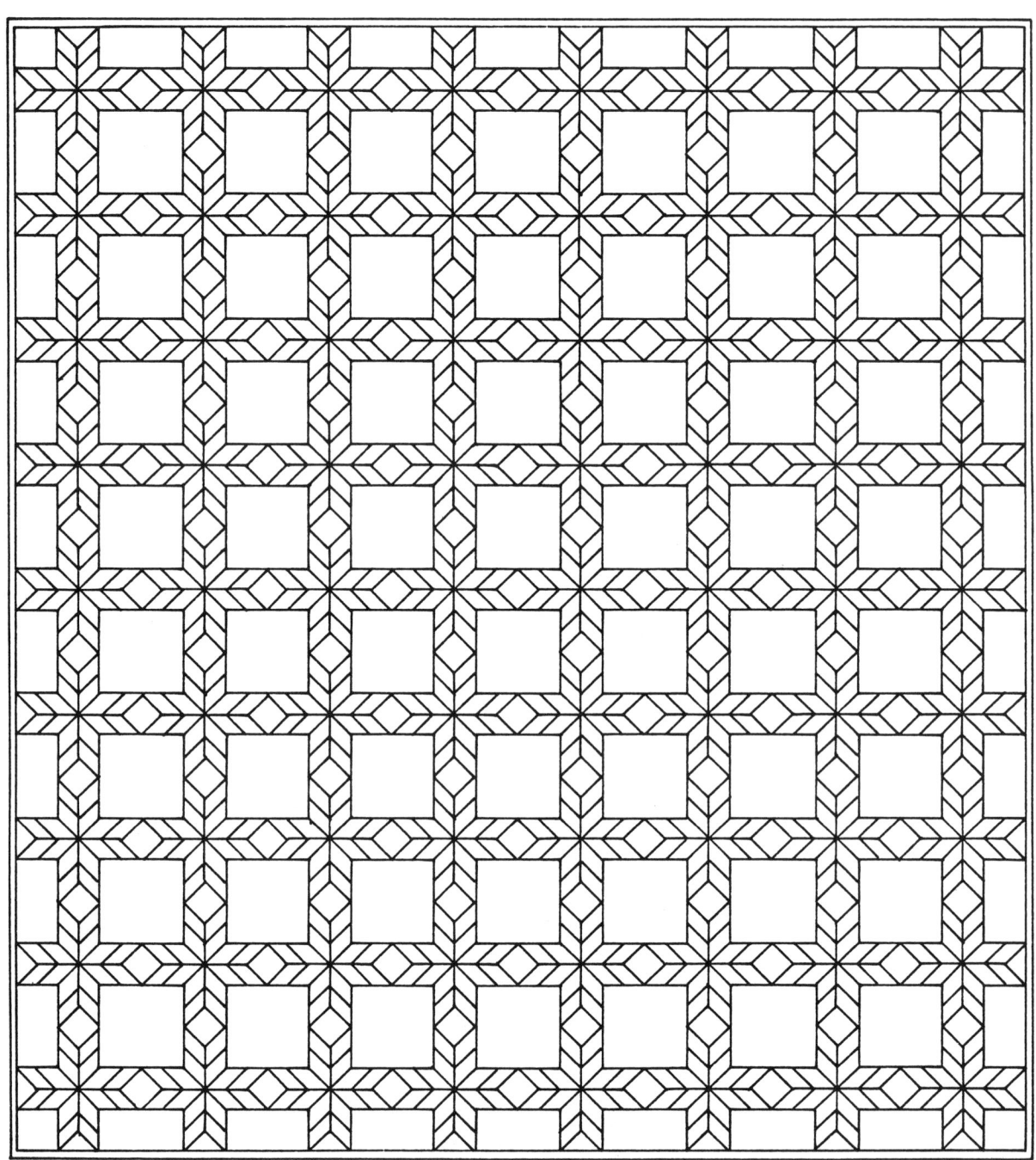

Touching Stars

Variable Stars

Double Star

Evening Stars

Hexagonal Stars

Star Variation

Broken Star

Feathered Star center

Star of Bethlehem

Blazing Star

Star Variation

Feathered Stars

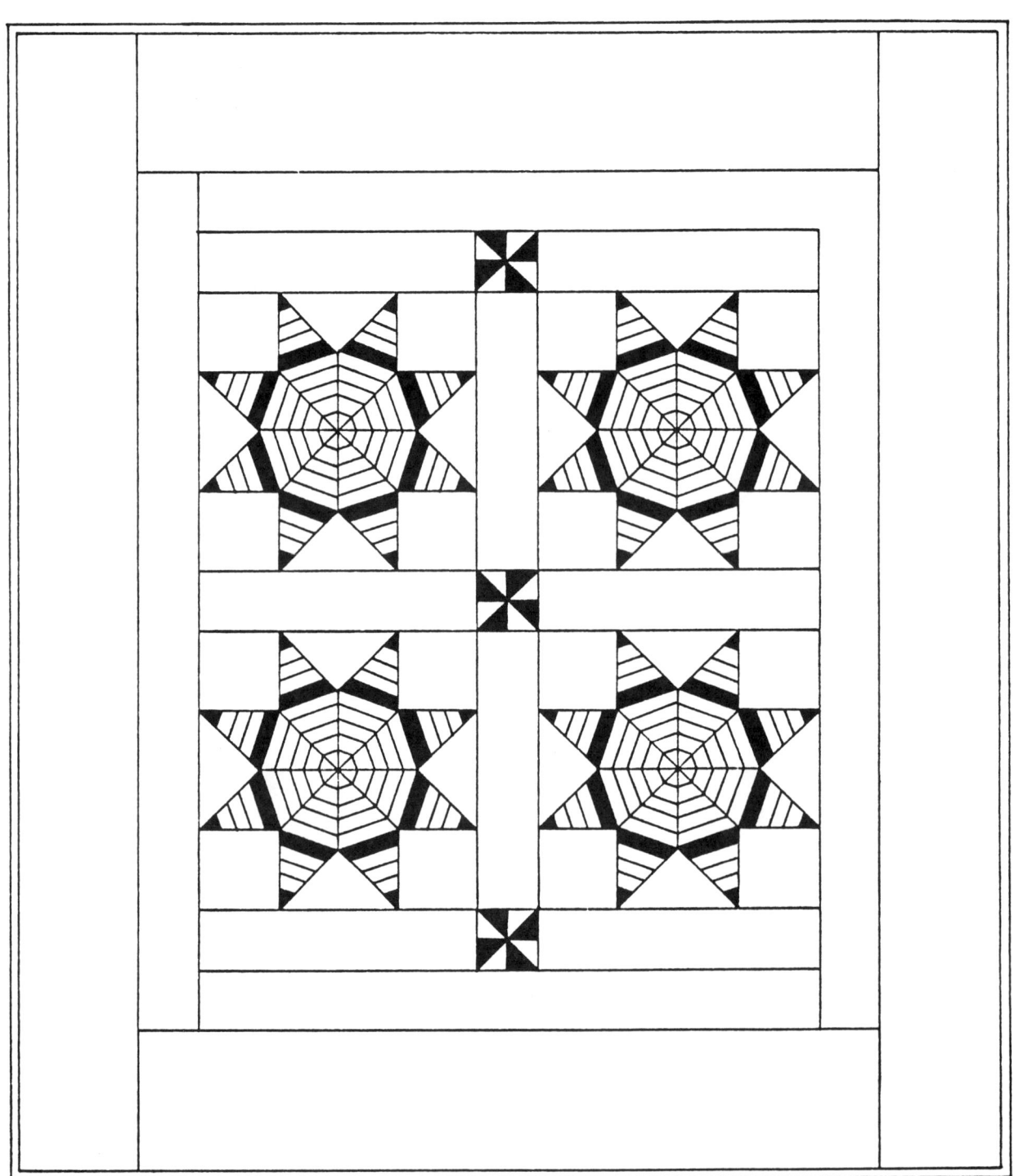

Spiderweb Stars

Stars and Leaves

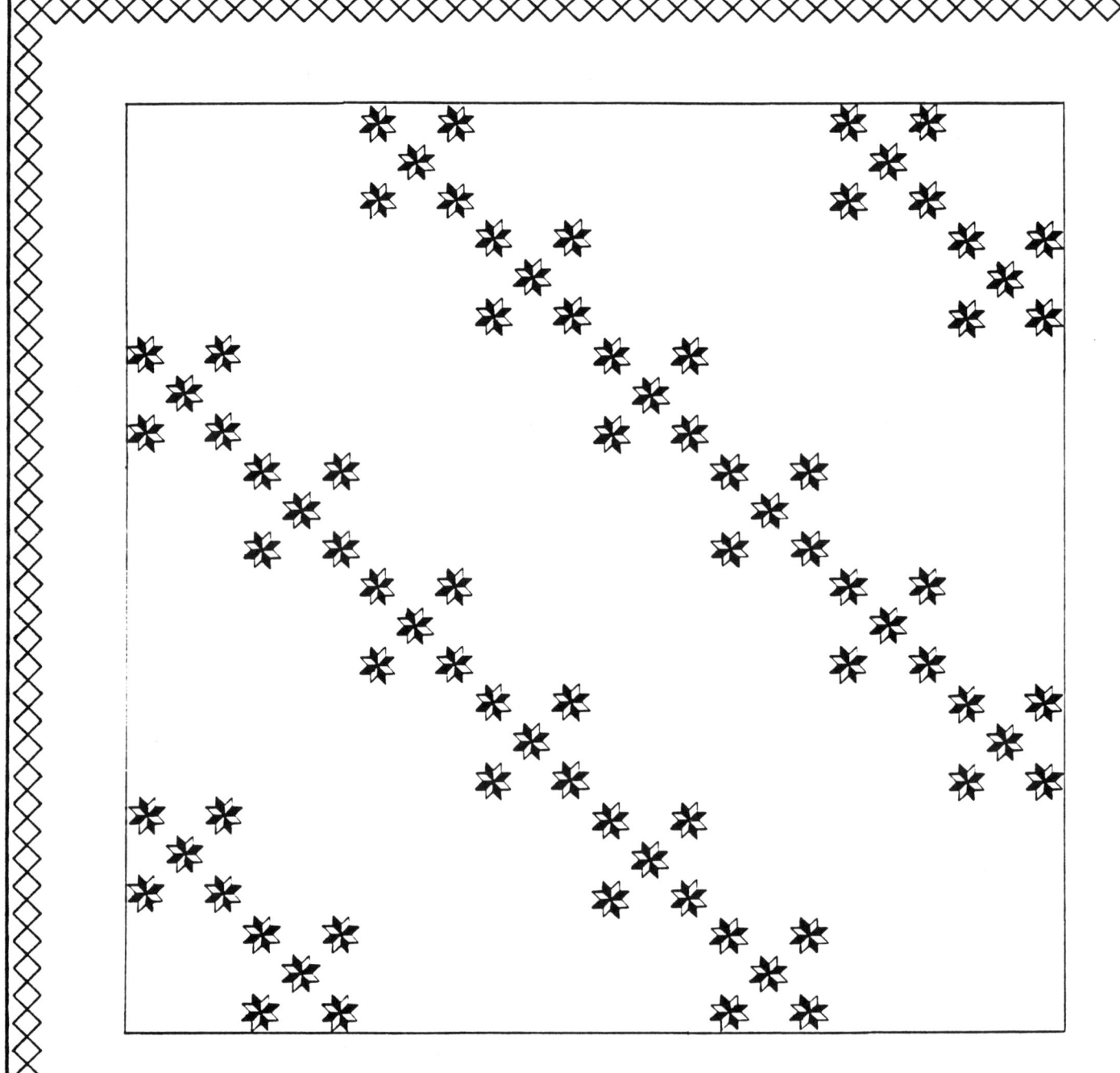

Lemon Stars

***Star of Bethlehem
with pieced borders***

Northumberland Stars Variation

Variable Stars Variation

Le Moyne Stars and Pinwheels

Rising Sun

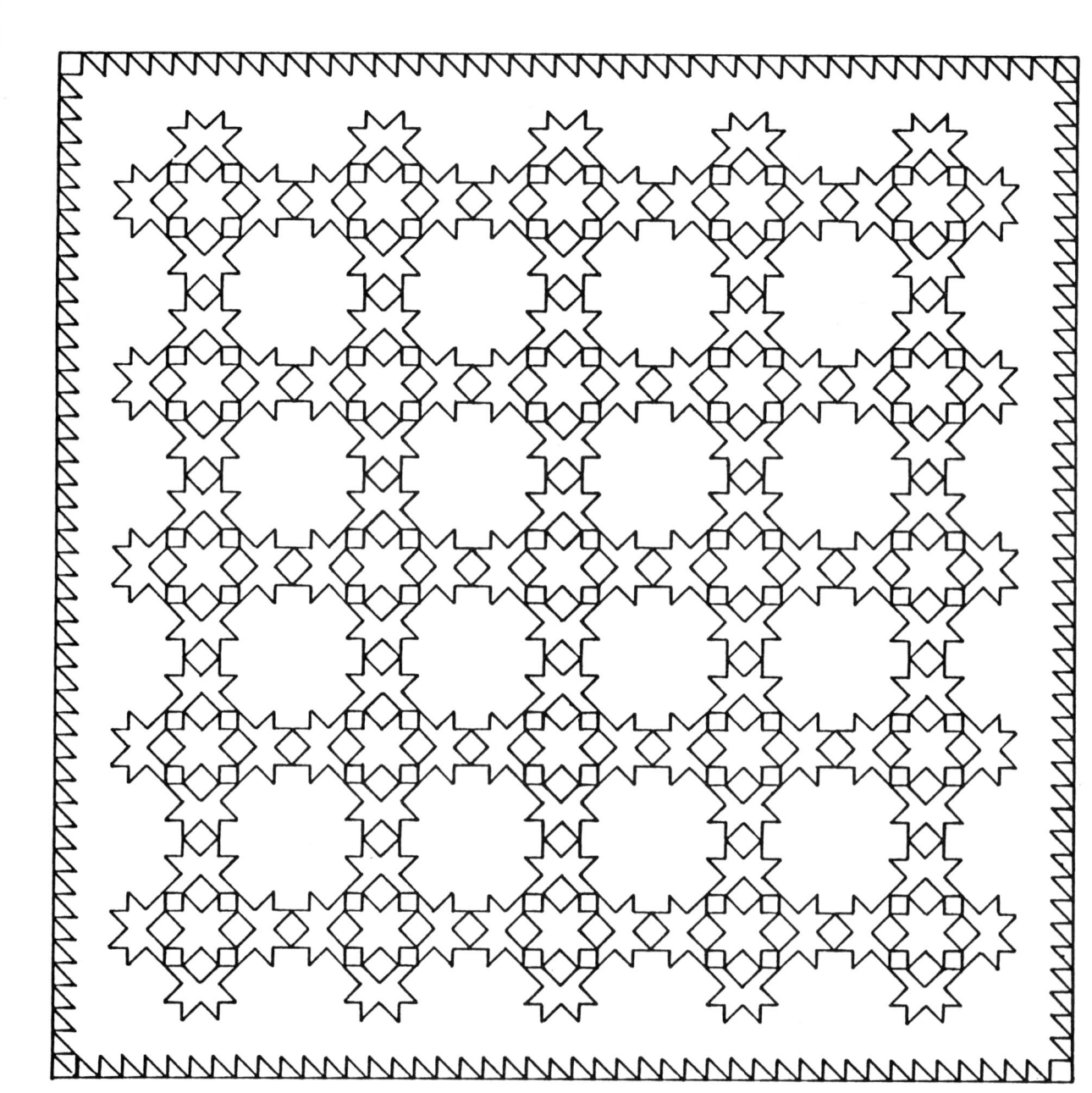

Heavenly Stars

Le Moyne Stars

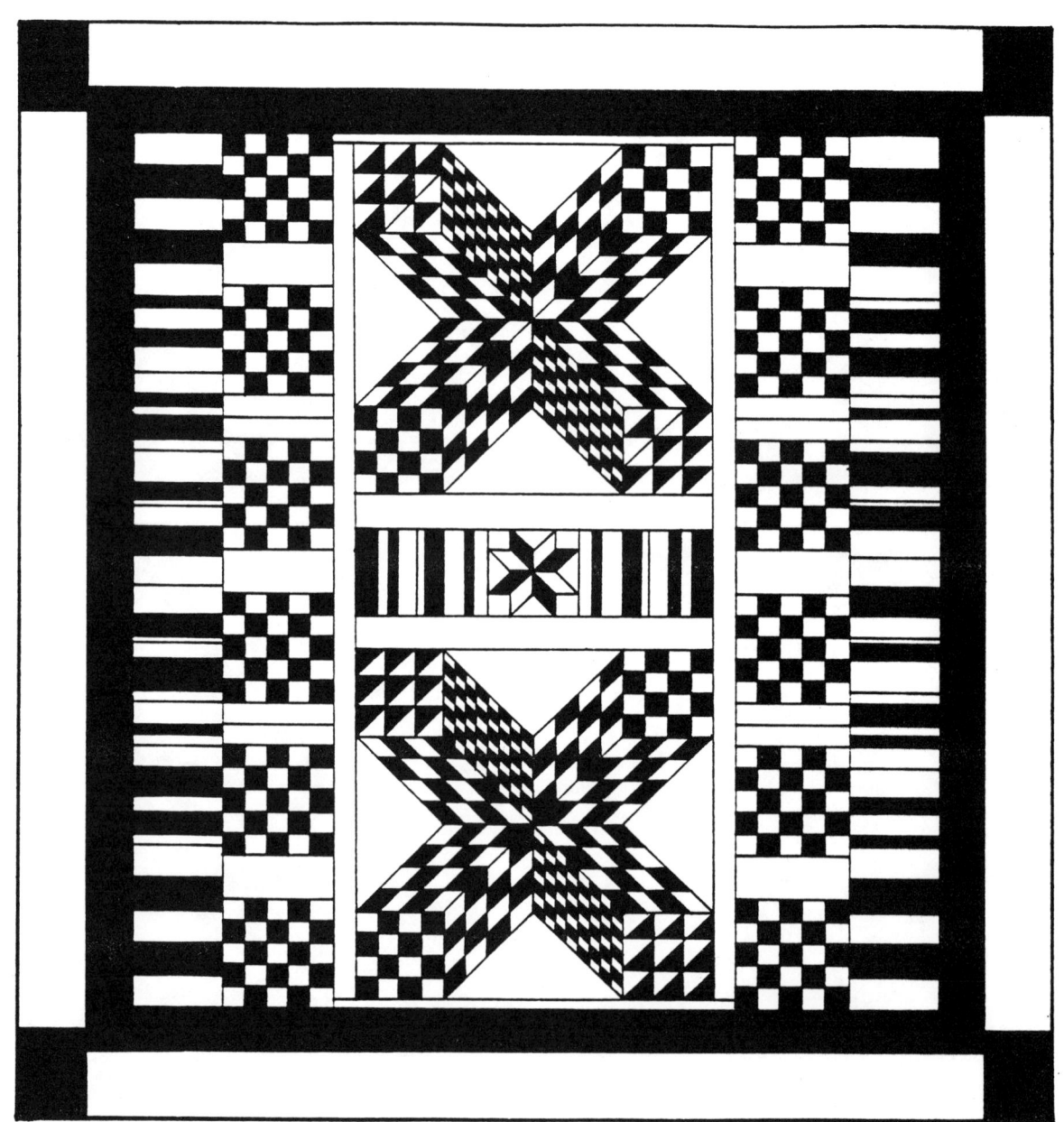

Star Variation

Star of France

Four-Pointed Stars

Feathered Star with floral appliqués

Star of Bethlehem

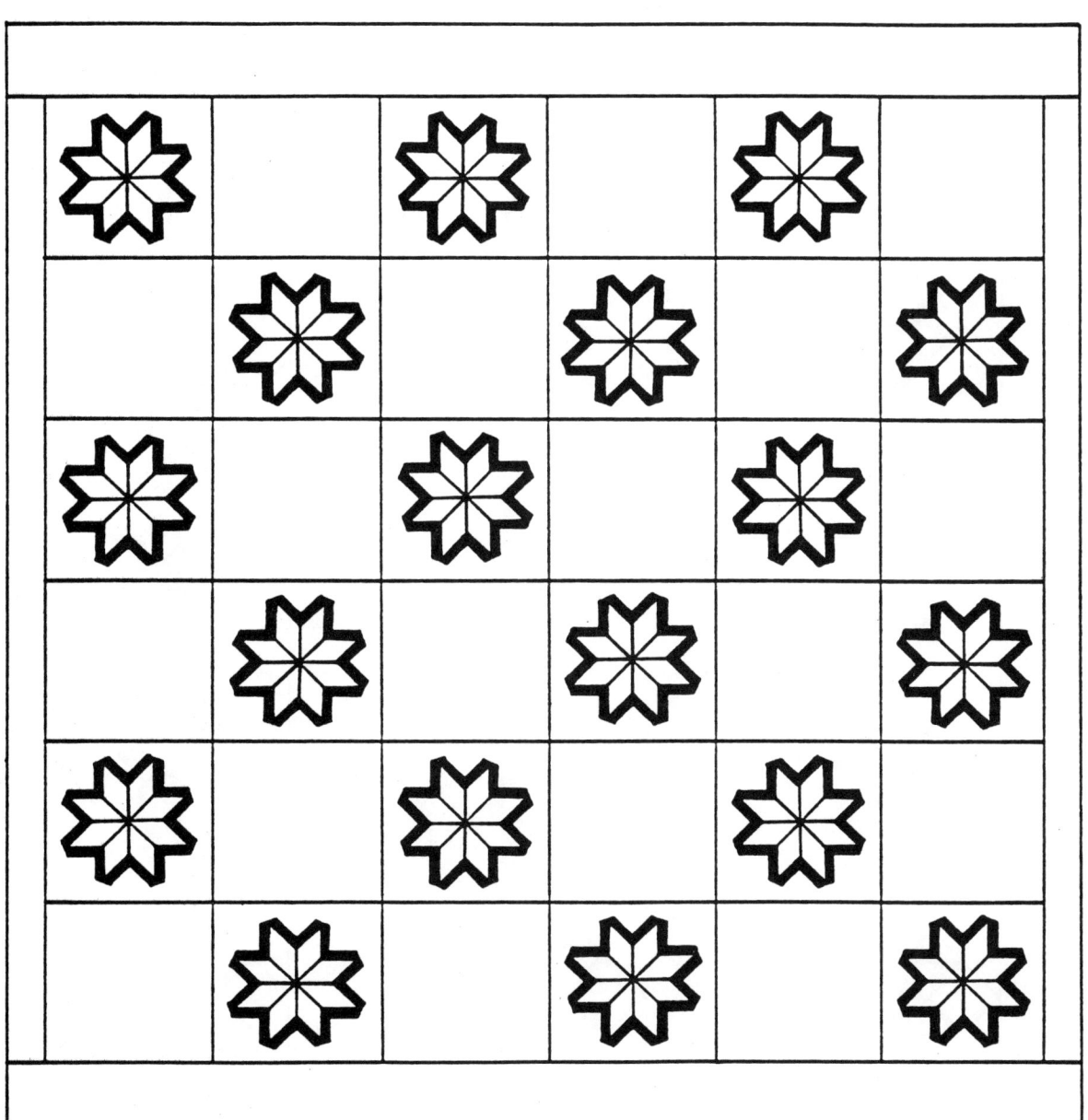

Lucinda's Star

Crystal Stars

Star Sampler

Star of the East

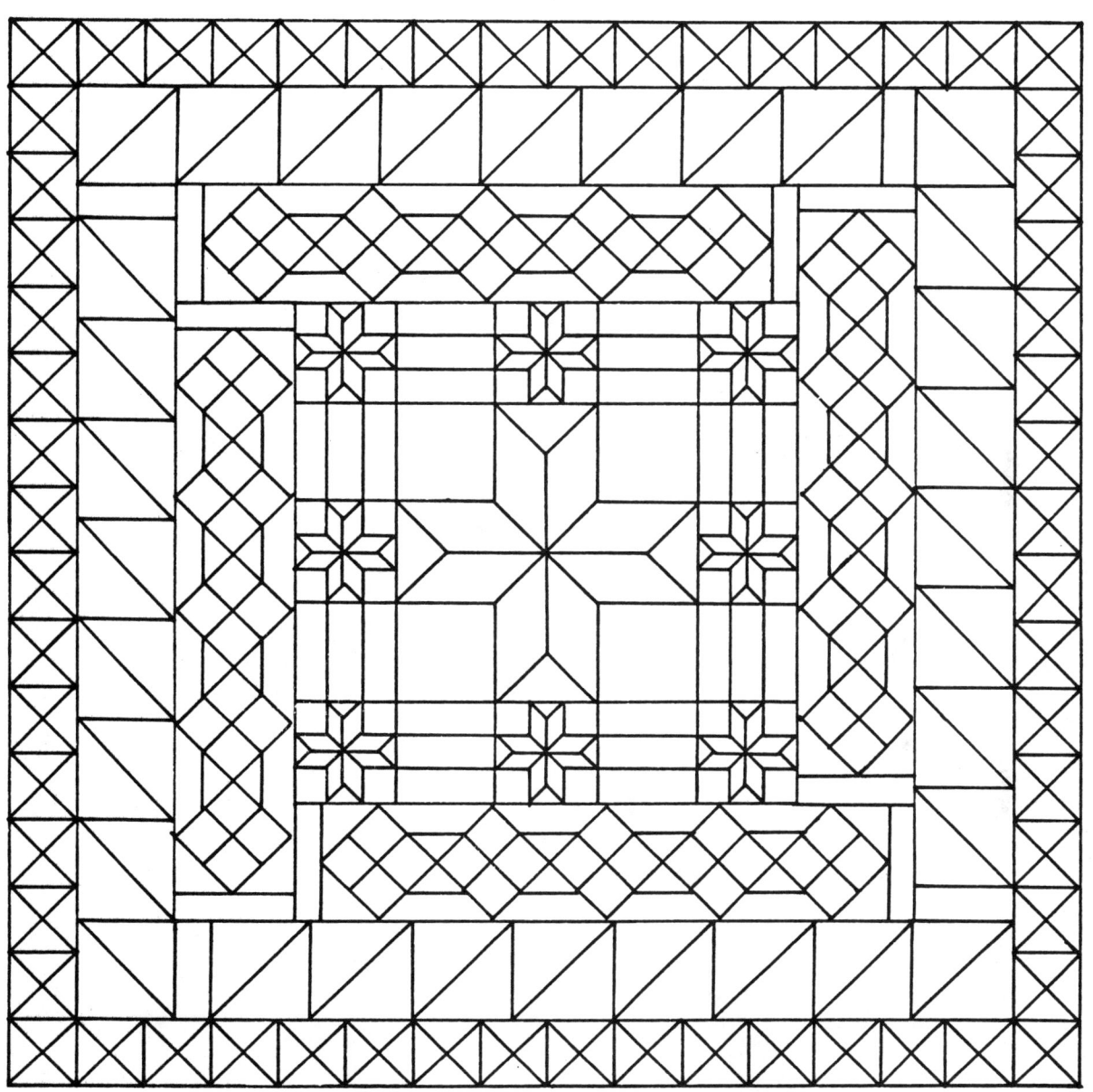

Eight-Pointed Star Medallion

Pieced Star

34

Le Moyne Stars

Star of Bethlehem

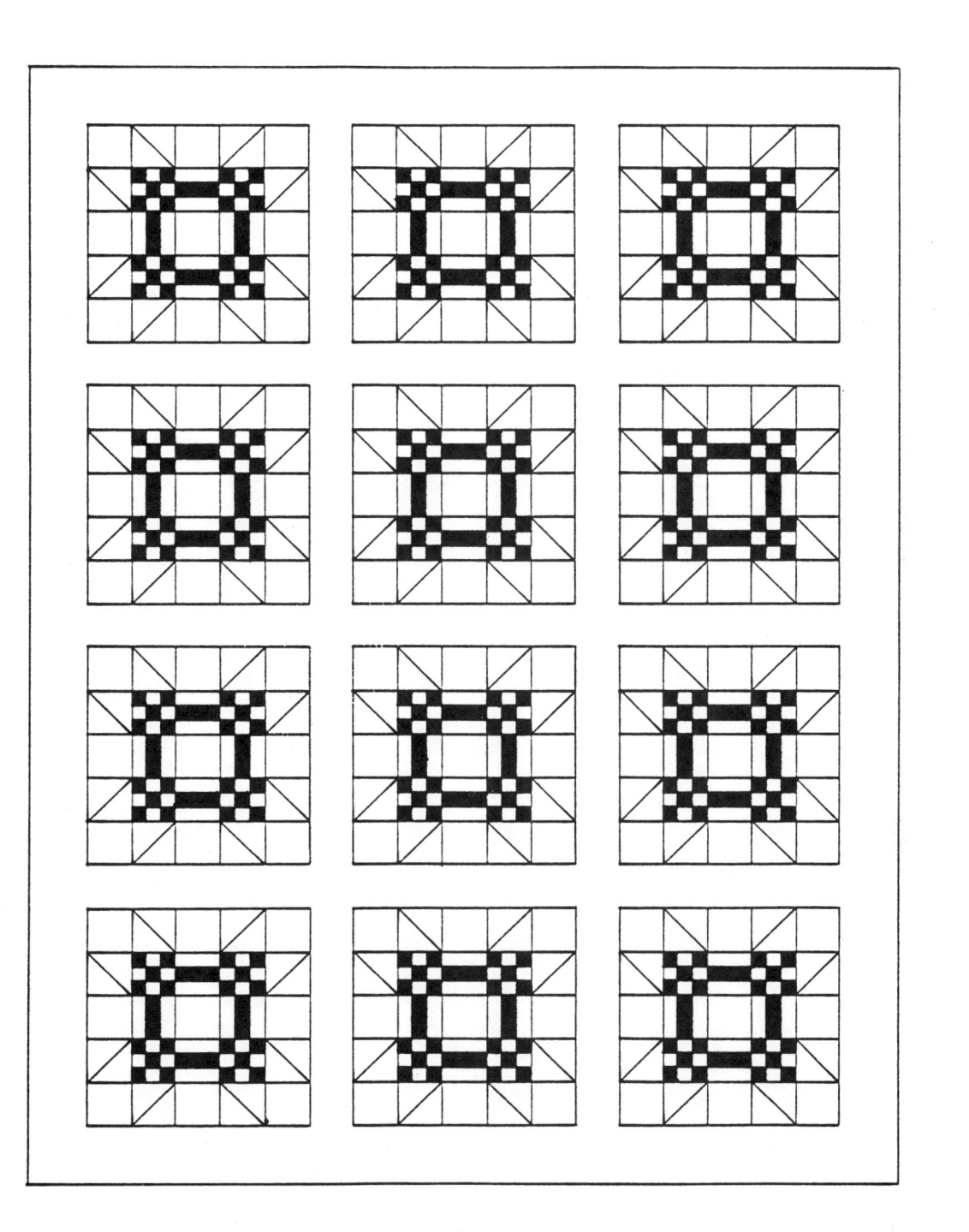

David and Goliath Variation

Five-Pointed Stars

Star Burst

Prairie Stars

Evening Star Medallion

Star of Bethlehem with Variable Star border

Variable Star with Sawtooth borders

Liberty Stars